THE
Nook
BOOK

HOW TO CREATE AND ENJOY
THE COZIEST SPOT IN THE HOME

Karen Hansgen

Clarkson Potter/Publishers
New York

Copyright © 2003 by Clarkson Potter

Published by Clarkson Potter/Publishers, New York, New York
Member of the Crown Publishing Group, a division of Random House, Inc.
www.randomhouse.com

CLARKSON N. POTTER is a trademark and POTTER and colophon are
registered trademarks of Random House, Inc.

Printed in Singapore

Design by Caitlin Daniels Israel

Library of Congress Cataloging-in-Publication Data
Hansgen, Karen.
The nook book : how to create and enjoy the coziest spot in the home / Karen Hansgen.—1st ed.
p.   cm.
Includes index.
1. Room layout (Dwellings).   2. Interior decoration.   3. Personal space.   I. Title.
NK2113 .H26 2003
747—dc21   2002153334

ISBN 1-4000-4732-3

10   9   8   7   6   5   4   3   2   1

First Edition

For my mother

ACKNOWLEDGMENTS

Thanks to the photographers, who provided their wonderful images. Thanks also to my friends at Clarkson Potter: Caitlin Daniels Israel, for her elegant design; Ronnie Grinberg, for all her hard work; and especially Annetta Hanna, for her inspiration. And finally, thanks to Emmett, who brings me coziness every day.

A commodious U-shaped booth has been inserted at the window of this urban kitchen. Covered in soft and practical vinyl in eye-pleasing chocolate and banana, the seat provides plenty of room for family and friends. An extra diner-style table can be pushed in for more surface space when needed.

CONTENTS

INTRODUCTION

We all have fondly remembered nooks from childhood—a specially selected hiding spot, a closet fort, a bunk bed, a refuge as simple as a blanket thrown over a couple of chairs. As adults, we still seek out a special hideaway in our homes, whether it's a favorite window seat for petting the cat, a quiet nook for reading the paper, a canopied bed for stealing a nap, or an alcove for enjoying a leisurely Sunday breakfast.

Anyone can create a secluded or sheltered place in his or her home, a sanctuary for relaxation and reflection. This microclimate can be as simple or elaborate as one likes, and designed with any style in mind: Victorian, country, deco, modern, contemporary—all will work; it depends simply upon the taste of the individual or family. A nook can be created in an existing small space or by setting a section of a room apart with even the most ordinary of objects: A screen can define an area, and that place can be made more intimate with personal items; drapery not only softens transitions between rooms but also can create a separate space. Enough room and an ample window are all one needs to install a breakfast nook in the kitchen. And a little imagination can go a long way to adding built-ins to a child's room that not only produce a fantasyland for younger children, but also can come apart and be reassembled to grow with them as they enter adolescence and then the teenage years.

A customized nook can be not only beautiful and serene, but functional, too: A home office in the form of a tucked-away desk in a landing; a sewing nook nestled into the gable of a renovated attic room; a bar built under a staircase. All it takes are thoughtful construction and the appropriate provisions.

The architecture of a home provides the most easily accessed nooks. Victorian houses, for example, offered a number of nooks for embellishing, with their sloping rafters, gables, and eaves and their angled bay windows. Even as decorating styles evolved, the nook remained integral to

PREVIOUS SPREAD Borrowing from the influence of Turkey, this hedonistic hideaway can be achieved by screening a small room behind a carved wooden partition and then layering it with an abundance of cushy pillows, carpets, and blankets in varied textures and exotic hues. Here lush tones of rose dominate the silk-covered pillows with silk fringe and the fabric-covered walls, which further soften and warm this enticing room.

———•———

home design. In the early twentieth century, more open and flexible spaces were favored, as natural wood and simple designs replaced the excesses and formality of Victorian design. The Arts and Crafts Movement of the late nineteenth and early twentieth centuries was in large part a reaction to the ornate and heavy style of the Victorian era. In Gustav Stickley's Craftsman houses, the living room replaced the parlor and the fireplace became the center of the home. Around the Craftsman hearth were built-in bookshelves and benches called inglenooks. Plans for Stickley homes, with their many practical nooks, were made available to the public. These houses became quite popular in the first half of the twentieth century. Their interiors emphasized form as well as function, and the built-in design elements gave these homes a sense of unity.

A nook doesn't have to be part of your home's architecture, however. In the following pages you will discover inventive ways to create your own niche or alcove for work, domestic tasks, and relaxation.

RIGHT This tub enclosure soaks
up sun from the skylight above,
with the glow of the light and the
comfort of a round bath inviting
one to linger—a rare luxury in our
fast-paced lives. Natural beige
ceramic tile absorbs the sun and
enhances the feeling of warmth.
The broad ledge around the tub is
a perfect home for a plant, such as
this orchid, as it receives plenty of
filtered light and humidity.

FAR RIGHT A plump mattress
placed on a raised platform of
tongue-and-groove paneling
creates a sheltered retreat in this
sleeping alcove, made cozier still
by a plush down duvet, a candle,
and soft blue walls. Wrought iron
is used as a design motif that
carries through the decorative
headboard, which is attached to
the wall, the candlestick, the
curtain rods, and the base of the
drafting table.

CHAPTER ONE

The kitchen has become the center of the contemporary family's life. Not only the place where meals are prepared and eaten, this room also serves as a communications center and command post, where schedules are posted on the fridge door, bills are paid, homework is done, and stories are shared.

What could be more inviting and convenient than a sunny breakfast nook as the hub of all this activity?

Dining rooms in family homes originated in England during the Georgian era as symbols of wealth. Before that, meals were eaten in the kitchen, close to the warmth of the hearth. The Arts and Crafts Movement provided an inadvertent return to this arrangement. But the move back from dining room to kitchen wasn't just about fashion, it was also about lifestyle. In the period between the two World Wars, factories employed more workers and offered better wages, so there were fewer household servants than there had been in the past. Out of necessity, homes had to be easier to maintain. Serving meals in the kitchen was more convenient for the housewife, who was now managing most of the household tasks on her own.

The built-in breakfast nook became common in American homes of the 1920s and 1930s. Sears, Roebuck and Co. and Montgomery Ward, among others, sold prefab house-building kits that included breakfast nooks, usually consisting of two benches at a table, often at a window. The nook came to be used for far more than the morning meal, however; it also provided a place for other activities throughout the day, from doing homework with children to playing evening card games and enjoying snacks.

As years passed and tastes changed, kitchens were remodeled and many nooks were lost. But these lost nooks, and their charm, can often be easily restored, if you have enough space. You can also install a new breakfast nook or remodel one that looks dated. Breakfast nooks should always be practical. You can add extra storage by flanking a table with benches that are constructed with hinged tops, thereby creating space to stash table linens, art supplies for the kids, or magazines. Seat backs can double as shelves for books or a collection of bowls or pitchers on the other side.

PREVIOUS SPREAD Like having your cake and eating it too, this captivating corner is both a window seat and a dining nook. It's a modernist's dream, and one you can make come true if you're lucky enough to have a corner of windows. Platform seats built along these windows not only look great, but they're also an efficient use of space. Fruit-filled Danish Krenit bowls add an appealing touch of color.

If you don't have the space in your kitchen for a built-in, there are other ways to achieve a dining area with a warm, nooklike feeling. Stenciled walls or patterned wallpaper can set apart a space adjacent to the kitchen. So can a thoughtfully placed screen or cleverly hung curtains. You might want to incorporate a style motif, such as log cabin rustic or colorful 1950s Americana. A bench or church pew from a flea market can be cushioned and serve as a banquette. Just add some chairs across the table and you have a nook.

If you need some space flexibility, a drop-leaf table can be accommodating. Keep it small for breakfast and widen it when you have a big project and need to spread out lots of books and papers. The important thing is that it be an inviting place to sit and relax, whether for a meal or a long talk with a friend.

Capturing the comfort of nostalgia, this dining nook has been outfitted with a Formica table and chairs, an old-fashioned corner china cabinet, and retro collectibles. Going all out with a 1950s south-of-the-border theme like this one is a sure way to set a little room apart. The playful color scheme, along with the mix of patterns in the wallpaper and the linoleum flooring, keeps things festive.

Well-chosen chairs, along with color and scale, are important considerations in creating your dining nook. LEFT A dining room uses bright colors and a 1950s Americana motif. A picket fence and a simple retro valance are used as window treatments. Other collectibles, such as the vintage tablecloth over a Formica table, assist in fashioning a delightful space for a Sunday breakfast of homemade waffles or an afternoon snack of deep-dish cherry pie.

a delightful space for a
Sunday
breakfast

LEFT The "shabby chic" flea market hodgepodge of furniture, paintings, and collectibles from different periods and places works in part because of the green and orange color scheme. The ivy wallpaper–covered screen encloses the area and can make this dining nook even more intimate, depending on how it is positioned. One easy way to create a screen is to wallpaper three basic plywood doors found at any lumberyard and then attach them with hinges.

RIGHT Classic Windsor chairs painted white flank a wooden table that has been freshly topped with a marble slab, making it more kitchen-friendly. The pimiento-stained straight-back bench, rescued from a rummage sale, makes this dining area feel like a nook.

BELOW An exuberant corner of a Southern California kitchen takes advantage of the region's abundant sunshine. A well-cushioned bench alongside one wall makes it a delightful nook. Influenced by the Mediterranean, the bleached white and deep azure blue of the walls and windowpanes complement the brightly colored throw pillows, which echo the colors of the fruit in the still life painting.

ABOVE When dining at a restaurant, people often request a booth because it's cozy and intimate. If you have the space, why not build one in your own kitchen? This beautifully crafted custom-made dining booth in a New York City apartment is roomy in that it can accommodate many people, but its efficient design means that it doesn't take up a lot of space.

RIGHT This lively dining alcove was conceived around an impressive collection of Fire-King dishware prominently displayed on the built-in shelves that layer the walls. If you have a cherished collection, consider showing it off with bracket shelves like these, which are easy to install. All that is required are brackets, boards, and paint—available at any big hardware store. The stenciled windowsill, brightly painted ladder-back chairs, and retro tablecloth all embellish the style and characteristic color of the Fire-King.

Remnants of a discarded picket fence lend a feeling of country comfort to this breakfast room. The homemade furniture was found at a flea market, but it could be crafted at home with the right supplies. Deep cushions and throw pillows affectionately covered in vintage florals, checks, and plaids will make it hard for you to get to work on time. Aprons are cleverly employed as drapery.

BELOW Curtaining off a section of a larger room is an obvious way to create a nook. A meringue-colored portiere both divides this living room and dining room and unites them, as it carries one of the design motifs, wrought-iron ornamentation. The sculptural table and chairs have a playful, contemporary feel.

ABOVE An antique wicker daybed from the early twentieth century that's generously tossed with needlepoint- and chintz-covered pillows helps give this tearoom its charm. The old wicker works well with the faded table and mismatched chairs. Another integrative element in this room is the use of soft spring colors from the garden.

The inherent warmth of wood plays a major role in these dining nooks. Here something as simple as a bookcase serves as a room divider with the added advantage of providing vacant space above to keep things feeling open. The sun-soaked butter yellow dining area boasts a sturdy oak table and chairs.

BELOW The built-in breakfast nook, with its shelves and telephone nearby, can also serve as a home office. The old farm table, wooden chairs with rush seats, and decorative baskets lend a homey feel to this alcove.

ABOVE Architect Frank Lloyd Wright's built-in shelving units and breakfast rooms were instrumental elements in achieving the open and flowing spaces he is famous for. In almost all of his kitchens, no matter the size, a breakfast nook was included. Here ledges around the brick wall house collections of small bronze sculptures and pottery by Ed and Mary Scheier.

LEFT With its exquisitely carved wooden arch and low teak table, this tearoom imported from Indonesia is elegant and exotic. Simple upholstered seat cushions are placed on the floor, flanking the table on three sides. The cubicle is small enough to be tucked into the corner of an obliging room or even a large hallway. Keep in mind that floor pillows call for flexibility, so let's hope your guests haven't been skipping out on their yoga classes. RIGHT A table and two old chairs with rattan seats are tucked under the stairs in this rustic cabin. A collection of tinware, metal placards of ads, and other paraphernalia from the 1940s is prominently displayed in and on every serviceable niche and surface. All of the items in this homespun nook can be found in American flea markets. Start collecting now.

ABOVE AND LEFT This hardworking kitchen corner is not only comfortable and appealing, but it is utilitarian as well. A banquette is installed around a corner. The softly cushioned benches are hinged, opening to abundant storage space underneath. Built-in shelves above hold everything from cookbooks to collectibles. The drop-leaf wooden table is versatile, stretching to different sizes, and it's practical—spilled juice, Magic Markers, and mugs of hot tea can do no real damage to its pleasantly worn surface.

30

Deep scarlet and oak enliven the friendly breakfast corner of this little kitchen. The chairs, lace-edged shelves, and many of the dishes and adornments are from the 1920s. Lighter hues are a typical choice when painting the kitchen, but more ardent colors can work beautifully in a small space.

A sturdy butcher-block table plays two roles in this small kitchen. Slide the tall stools underneath the block when you need a work surface, pull them out when it's time for dinner. Pale marble countertops, cream-colored cabinets, and balloon shades look striking against the mango-colored walls. A large mirror makes the space feel roomier.

The color scheme of this compact room is cool and pleasing. The high table and chairs in pale teal impart a feeling of elevation. If you have a small area to work with and like an uncluttered look, consider using light colors and tall furnishings such as these to draw the space up. Perfectly polished stainless-steel pots are reflected in a mirror panel, which also extends the space.

Most of us have an inherent impulse to nest, and in our homes we gravitate toward a favorite nesting place. If you are lucky enough to have a built-in window seat, then you probably recognize its value as a place for retreat. What could be more pleasurable than an afternoon spent lounging, reading, and gazing out a window?

Having a comfortable place to sit by a window also offers the benefits of natural light, which brightens anyone's mood.

If your home is not furnished with a window seat, it is not difficult to install one. Not only does a window seat provide an inviting retreat and add a unique architectural element to a room, but it also can supply much-needed storage space with cabinets underneath or shelves supporting the seat on either side. One easy way to construct a multipurpose window seat is by using sturdy prefab wall cabinets as the base of your window seat and prefab bookcases at either end. Then just add a seat cushion and toss on some pillows. Keep in mind that you will probably want this window seat ample enough to allow you to change positions—to sit up and write, recline and read, cuddle with a child, or have a cup of tea while lost in thought. Your seat should have a standard chair height of 16 inches, and be at least 12 inches in depth. The deeper the seat, the more inviting it will be. If the window seat is also going to serve as a lounge, you'll want to extend that depth to 24 inches, and to 38 inches for a daybed, which will comfortably accommodate an adult.

How to decorate this unique spot comes down to preference and personality. Perhaps you want to feel comforted here. Nostalgia and motifs from the past can provide an escape from the stress of the present and lend a sense of well-being. Certain pillows or fabrics can be comforting because they're reminiscent of childhood memories, such as visits to your grandmother's house. If you find a contemporary, minimal feel more soothing, squared cushions covered in a textured fabric of a single favorite color might be an apt choice.

Maybe you would like the space to be suggestive of fondly remembered travels abroad—to colorful India or Morocco, or serene Japan. When decorating this special spot, keep in mind those elements that appeal most to you. Create something that reflects your own tastes and pleasures, for this is a place to linger.

ABOVE Think beyond the limitations of a small space. This window seat/daybed makes good use of a sunny corner. A futon is placed on top of a raised platform of standard cabinets. It is covered in simple white with plush velour pillows in soft pastels thrown on top.

PREVIOUS SPREAD A place for the minimalist to dream, this built-in window seat is but a platform with two seamless white cushions and pillows on top. The crisp lines are accented by the striped throw rug in neutral tones. A blue vase filled with yellow wild flowers adds the perfect touch of extra color. A sheer window treatment diffuses the light.

LEFT The original architecture of this Cape Cod house included a built-in box of a window seat on either side of the fireplace. If you have a fireplace, chances are you have the space on either side to build a similar nook. Needlepoint- and gingham-covered pillows add to the appeal.

OPPOSITE If you have a large landing in your stairwell, one resourceful use of that area is to build a window seat that can double as a daybed. A mix of patterns and colors works well here with the unifying and soothing wall color. The liberal proportions of the cushioned surface beckon you to take a break on the way up the stairs, or even to steal a nap.

Perhaps the best part of a window seat is the pleasure of soaking up sunlight. Fortunately, fabricating a place in the sun does not have to be a complicated task. **BELOW** Built-in cabinetry and two bureaus support a window seat, which is topped with two standard-sized cushions. **RIGHT** A graceful window seat with thick damask curtains, embroidered pillows, and paneled shutters is composed of an upholstered bench pressed flush against the windows.

OPPOSITE A refuge at the bottom of the stairs allows for resting and nesting. Built-in drawers can hold magazines, books, and other items that tend to travel from floor to floor. The ample windowsill allows enough room for a cup of coffee, a snack, and even some pretty daffodils.

Think about the kind of mood you want your window seat to evoke. The finely finished wood, the pearl gray tones of the cushion and silk pillows, and the graceful statuary add an air of tranquillity to this window seat, which was inspired by a trip to Thailand. The serenity this seat provides, along with the alluring outdoor scenery, can make it a great place to escape to for minutes and even hours.

Having a window seat near a fireplace just might make life seem complete. The subtle diamond-patterned walls of this room in an English country cottage are as pleasing as the down throw pillows and sage green of the seat cushion. On a frosty winter day, the pillows can be moved to the floor so one can get even closer to the heat of the fire.

a restful place
to gaze out
the window

A wooden bench wraps
around the windows of this
sunroom in a weekend
house. The simplicity of this
seat allows it to be used as a
table, a place to set things,
extra seating for dinner
guests, or just a restful place
to gaze out the window.

When building your window seat, think of the many ways you might use it. With the right proportions and thick, supportive seat cushions, it can double as a bed for napping or for accommodating overnight guests. The window seat in this contemporary home has the added advantage of skylights above for extra sunlight during the day and stargazing at night.

One of the greatest benefits of large windows is that they allow you to bring the outdoors inside. This room feels like a garden with its green trelliswork-patterned wallpaper, flowery curtains, and wicker rocker. Drawers line the base of the window seat, providing the perfect place for storing linens, towels, or seasonal clothing.

In this English-style sitting room, the bay windows yield a passageway from indoors to the garden outside. Here the seat is used for plants and a telephone and a single round pillow is tossed on top for some comfort. Wicker chairs and screens contribute to the atmosphere of this charming nook.

If you have the space, why not add an extra place to idle in the bedroom? LEFT A mini-seat, nestled between two bureaus, can be used as a perch while you put on your shoes, or for your child to sit and read to you while you get ready in the morning. For a fresh look, mix patterns and textures, such as these tones of beige and blue. OPPOSITE The spectacular view from the window seat in this master bedroom provides the perfect transition from dreaming to waking. The seat is a great excuse for dawdling or stargazing before tucking in for the night. The opening of this seat is framed in finely detailed millwork with pocketed, raised panel window shutters; the cushion is covered in handsome plaid. The seat hides the baseboard-heating element below.

the perfect transition from
dreaming to
waking

Small children are always seeking out a secret spot or contained area, a hidden domain they can call their own. Think about what children do when presented with an oversized cardboard box; they resourcefully convert it into a fort to hide or play in. A step above a cardboard box is a creative built-in, which can be transformed into a playful nook.

Built-ins have the added advantages of being safe and versatile, and they're a great way to maximize storage and minimize clutter. Adaptable units can grow with your child from the nursery through the learning years, when their room functions as a play area, a library, and an art studio all at once; to early adolescence, when personal space and escape are important; and finally to the headstrong teen years, when privacy is desired above all else.

New parents sometimes go to great

lengths to furnish a nursery in anticipation of the precious new arrival. All that room needs, however, is a safe crib, an accessible changing area, and a comfortable spot for parents to sit during feedings. Not overburdening this room with furnishings that an infant will quickly outgrow provides much more flexibility.

As your child matures, his or her personality matures as well, and it's important to create a room as individual as the child who inhabits it. A room should evolve with the needs and interests of your child. Consider letting your child become involved in the design process, being careful to avoid trends and current favorites that will quickly grow tired. While you might be more timid in other rooms, this is your chance to experiment with bright and contrasting colors and bold and unusual patterns. Built-ins can always be painted over to adapt to your child's changing tastes.

Bunk beds are a sure hit with younger children, and they can provide creative solutions for small spaces. They are also a great way to provide individual territory when a room is shared by siblings. If a child has his or her own room, a bunk bed can accommodate sleepovers. In a family vacation home, multiple bunks are an effective use of space, providing sleeping space for family and guests.

Kids are natural multitaskers, so why not give them a room that does the same? Other creative, practical, and pleasant nooks for a child's room include window seats with added storage; loft beds that allow enough room for a desk, easel, and toy storage underneath; and built-in playhouses that can provide hours of imaginative fun. Burrowing comes naturally to children, and any chance you can give them to pursue this activity in their own room is sure to make that place more comfortable and welcoming.

ABOVE A ladder on wheels, with a curved guide rod, connects two tall bookshelves and the bunk bed in between. One of these shelves then acts as a wall for added solitude when needed for study at the sturdy built-in desk. While this is a large room, the way it is divided into niches makes it feel cozy, without sacrificing height or light.

PREVIOUS SPREAD It's a party. And a parade. Take the doors away and paint the closet red. Toys are not hidden away in a heavy chest but are accessible and shown off. If you have another closet where you can store your child's clothes, then think of using a closet in his or her room as an inviting niche for play. Lively wallpaper with running and tumbling children enhances the fun.

BELOW A day at the seashore is evoked by this room with its custom-built loft bed made to look like a lifeguard's tower. The lookout leaves lots of space underneath for play. A brightly striped awning for a curtain, carpet the color of soft sand, and walls painted with waves and a clear blue sky make this room feel like a trip to the beach. **OPPOSITE** Here is a safari adventure in the corner of a child's room. The painted jungle walls, complete with elephant and lion, set the mood. The built-in cabinet provides surface space on top for toys and pictures, and has storage space underneath as well. With a little advance planning, you can build that cabinet in proportions that allow you to repaint and transform the area into a window seat when your child gets older.

ABOVE Sports and the locker room are the inspiration for this fun room. Primary colors and broad stripes are in abundance. The locker door cabinets not only look great, but they also provide storage space for all of the bats, balls, and other equipment that your young athlete accumulates.

LEFT If two siblings share a bedroom, it's a good idea to give them individual workstations for completing homework. These built-in desks are divided by an architecturally inspired bookshelf, which serves the dual purpose of holding books and other objects and of separating the two young scholars so that they can concentrate on their schoolwork. OPPOSITE This playful corner looks like an aquarium, with the sea creatures on the watery wall spilling over onto the table and chairs. Children love being immersed in imaginative spaces like this one. Having a small table and chairs that accommodate their compact sizes is essential. When the theme starts to feel tired, fresh paint and a bigger table or desk provide instant transformation.

One way to set an area apart for imaginative play is to build a platform in your
child's room, which can serve as a stage, a
room in a game of house, or a podium for
an important speech. With its dreamy
colors, this fairy-tale castle theme may be
more appropriate for younger children,
but new paint and a change of curtains will
yield an easy update as a child matures.

A tea party, a Victorian rocking horse, a doll cradle filled with favorite friends, and a noble berth tucked into a magical garden—this dream room would cast a spell over any aspiring princess. While flamboyantly floral, the room is small enough to oblige the creeping ivy, fluttering birds, and flowers in full bloom. It stays cozy with its warm colors, soft rug, and comfy bed nestled in under the eave.

Tucked into the sloping rafters of an attic, this playroom provides plenty of space for fun and games. The soft satin-finished floors reflect the white ceiling, with both down lighting and natural light coming in through the oval window. Wallpaper with a classic yet playful pattern keeps things lively. Shelves with space for large toys are built to the specifications of the room.

The facade of a house, complete with architectural detail and a screen door, is
constructed over and around the doorway that separates these two rooms. Not only does
this imaginative treatment divide these two rooms, but it also inspires creative play.
Installing a desk along a wall with built-in shelves is practical and a great space saver. It
also provides a feeling of enclosure that can be conducive to more concentrated work.

Many older urban apartment buildings have high ceilings, but the rooms have shrunk over years of renovating and reconfiguring. This awkwardly shaped room is used to maximum benefit with an angled loft bed that leaves plenty of play space below. A dollhouse is perched on two small cupboards, leaving a gap in between that acts as a bookshelf. Raspberry may be a daring color choice, but it works in small doses and would tickle any little girl pink.

An attic conversion can be the perfect room for a child, who, after all, doesn't need a lot of headroom. When that child gets older, the same room will feel like a private refuge and personal space. If you're worried it might be too dark, add rooflights (windows in the flat plane of the roof). Thoughtful employment of color will also lighten up an attic space.

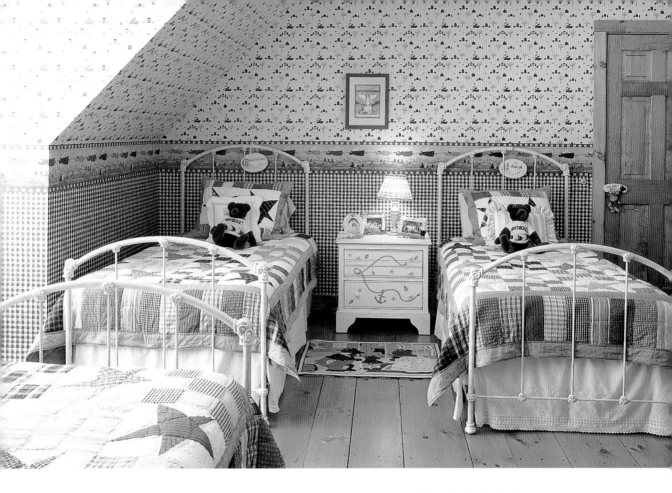

OPPOSITE The lavish use of purple would not disappoint a little girl. The high-gloss painted floor reflects the light coming in from above and further opens up the space.

ABOVE Quilts and a lively mix of patterns in the wallpaper animate an attic conversion in this beach house. Employing painted iron beds rather than solid wood headboards is a good choice because they allow light to pass through, making the space feel roomier.

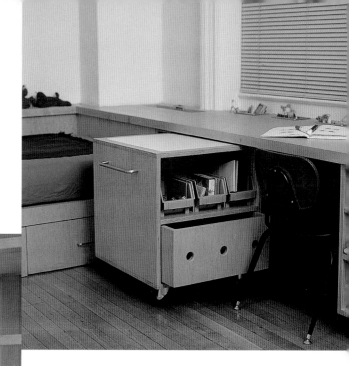

{ the look is clean
and minimal, allowing for
inevitable
clutter

OPPOSITE It's all a good fit in this smart room for siblings. A series of nooks and niches has been crafted out of chunky blond wood to serve many needs—bulletin boards, desks, beds and ladders, drawers and cubbies everywhere, and perhaps smartest of all, modular units on wheels that double as storage and surface space. The look is clean and minimal, allowing for the inevitable clutter. BELOW Bunk beds are a great way to accommodate friends and cousins in a weekend or summer retreat. The bottom bunks of these beds have handy drawers for storage but could conceivably be proportioned to hold trundle beds if more sleeping space is required. The recessed areas behind the bunks hold shelves for lamps and reading materials. That way the night owl can read quietly while others peacefully slumber.

A garage is converted into a lucky teenager's personal haven in this Los Angeles home. Built-in shelves, a desk, and a platform bed on top of a set of drawers maximize the use of the tight space. Utilizing a mostly monochromatic color scheme imparts a greater sense of fluidity in a small room. Not only will creating such a room help your teenager fulfill his or her demand for independence, but it will also give you a break from the sometimes unwelcome noise. Electric guitar? A loud stereo blasting? No problem.

CHAPTER FOUR

Perhaps the most important room in the home is the bedroom, since we spend a third of our lives there. In decorating this place of repose, one should give extra consideration to the bed, the spot where the day begins and ends. The bed is not just for sleeping, intimacy, and cuddling—it's a little world unto itself for retreat, and a perfect space for a variety of activities.

Rather than seek outside entertainment, many people cocoon in the haven of their homes. Couples come home from work late and hop into bed to eat takeout while watching a favorite TV show or movie, while families gather in bed to watch Saturday morning cartoons, to read the Sunday paper, and to share dreams. Not only are people spending more time in these mini-havens, but they're also spending more money on them, as evidenced by the many mail-order catalogs and specialty shops that are selling 500-plus-thread-count sheets, plush duvets, and exotic feather-stuffed pillows.

You can make your bedroom a sanctuary for relaxation and renewal. A bed with a canopy or curtains can become a separate world unto itself. Before window screens were invented, a canopy of netting was used for summertime sleeping by those who could afford the expensive fabric. This fabric encircled the entire bed and not only kept the bugs out, but also provided added privacy. In the winter, a thicker curtain was used to keep in body warmth. Today, a canopied look can be created with a frame, though not all rooms can accommodate a big four-poster bed. A solution for a smaller space might be to hang light, airy fabric from the ceiling.

Beds can be positioned creatively, giving a small bedroom new life. Building a platform for your bed overlooking the living room is an especially effective way to make good use of a tight urban space. A bed nestled into a converted attic corner provides extra privacy and intimacy. A loft bed is not only perfect for children, but it can be an island escape for adults as well. Tuck your bed under an eave and line the wall with soothing paper, enveloping yourself in warmth. Build a platform supported by three walls for a built-in bed that is sure to be cozy.

Also consider the bed in your guest room. A built-in daybed tossed with an abundance of pillows is inviting and provides extra storage space underneath. Having bookshelves with reading materials close by is a sure way to make overnight guests feel welcomed.

ABOVE Peel me a grape. The depth and breadth of this platform bed, along with its rich crimson and blond stripes, create a feeling of extravagance. Whether for lounging or sleeping, this retreat can be made even more private and intimate by pulling closed the curtains.

PREVIOUS SPREAD The pleasure of really tucking in at night is one you can achieve in your own home, as demonstrated by this platform bed with luxurious curtain enclosures. Close yourself off in your own little world, creating a room within a room. The map-patterned bedspread, seashells, and exotic animal etchings all lend to the sense of a getaway.

The very romantic look of this alcove is achieved primarily through the French provincial–printed cotton fabric used in the pretty drapery and bed skirt and on the walls. The landscape paintings enhance this bedroom's idyllic look. To imitate this feel at home, build a frame, tuck your bed inside, and cover the walls and bed with the fabric you most fancy. Sweet dreams.

If your tastes run to the eccentric, think about using a classic fabric in a bold color. Toile in vibrant poppy, white-washed walls and beams, dusky old portraits and whimsical landscapes, even the uneven terra-cotta tile on the floor all make for a fantastical but very dreamy retreat. Pull the curtain for ultimate privacy.

OPPOSITE This is what you can do with that extra and very tiny room in your apartment that was once the end of a hallway. Tuck a futon under the sunny window, toss it with cushy pillows covered in a variety of colors and patterns, and you have a nest for yourself or a lucky guest. BELOW A narrow loft built in the eaves serves as a sleeping area. The blond of the wood floor and white of the walls and unadorned bed make this a Spartan space indeed, but sometimes you want to be a recluse and give yourself away to good sleep. The round window acts like a painting. Other than that landscape, a single red anthurium adds the only touch of vivid color.

Resembling a Scottish boxbed, this mini-den provides welcome solace after a stressful day. An abundance of sturdy striped fabric wraps around every surface. Even the window can be covered for complete darkness. One large drawer has been tucked underneath the bed for storage.

BELOW Meditations on India animate this lavish bedroom. A carved screen is used as a window treatment. Reposition it and fashion a dressing area or further envelop the bed in the rich and dark wood. Contrasting with the floral magenta bedspread are an animal print pillow and stool, which add a touch of glamour.

ABOVE The dark wood, deep ruby velvet, and thick embroidery invite one to cocoon into the security of this Parisian nest. The swarthy textures and colors, the classic bouillotte lamp, game board, and carved lion on the card table, as well as the heavily framed pictures on the wall, give this a distinctly masculine feel.

BELOW This sleeping area is thoroughly Victorian with its crocheted lace sheets and pillow sham, handsomely framed etched portraits on floral wallpaper, checked bedspread and drapery, and chinoiserie pillow. This nostalgic look is achieved primarily through the use of fabric, something you can easily do at home. OPPOSITE A Gothic arch and deep rose paint set the sleeping alcove apart from the rest of this room. You can find architectural elements like this one at auctions and shops that specialize in such embellishments. Contemporary bed linens, a classical drawing, and a folk art painting of a rooster are juxtaposed in this eclectic mix of art and furniture styles.

{ secluded and *romantic*

Both extravagant and cozy, this
French Empire—inspired
corner of an artist's studio is
dominated by an ornate daybed
with silk damask bedding. The
elevated platform and draped walls
add to the drama, helping to set
this resting area apart from the
work space. Without the skylight,
the corner might feel dark and
cold, rather than secluded and
romantic.

OPPOSITE AND ABOVE A loft bedroom reflects the minimal modernism of the living room below with its simple yet elegant forms and cream and beige tones. Slim metal rods embedded in the ceiling hold up a wooden platform. Ledges with orchids and stainless-steel urns and cups act as a backboard and are just the right size for nighttime reading materials. This is a great idea for a tight urban space.

A quick getaway to your bed in the rafters. **ABOVE** In this cabin bedroom, white lace is a charming contrast to the rustic wood. The pitcher and bowl, the kerosene lamps, and the oval mirror aid in creating an old farmstead feel. **RIGHT** The use of all white can be both calming and exhilarating, as demonstrated by the bleached walls, beams, and roof trusses of this garret bedroom, which is complemented by the white bedding and sheer curtains. A rooflight in the pitched ceiling lets in plenty of sun.

If you like the idea of a canopy but your bedroom is too small to contain the drama of a four-poster bed, consider using a simple metal frame draped with a sheer fabric. Wispy gauze makes the room feel airy, as it sways with the breeze coming in through the windows or from the ceiling fan above.

With an abundance of fabrics to choose from, you can generate a variety of moods through the use of bed draperies. And a canopy does not necessarily have to be frilly and overtly feminine. Here three different treatments elicit different moods. **LEFT** Cotton voile gives this room a dreamy feel as it floats weightlessly from the ceiling, cornering this bed in comfort. **BELOW** Sheer muslin provides a contrast to the dark wood of the bed, and the profusion of light and a grass mat lend this room a safari feel. **OPPOSITE** A large sheath of organza, draped around and then suspended from the ceiling, is spectacular enough to carry this extravagant four-poster bed with an antique painted screen as a headboard.

CHAPTER FIVE

If you have an older, nonstandard home, it's probably full of special alcoves, uniquely shaped closets, and serviceable niches. Few homes being built today are equipped with these idiosyncratic areas, let alone a pantry, mudroom, or dressing room. If you live in a newer home or apartment where such spaces don't exist, there are, however, ways to create them.

Install a cushioned bench along a wall near the back or garage door and it can serve as a mudroom, where running shoes, garden clogs, and snow boots can be comfortably put on or taken off. Create a pantry along a back staircase by installing the proper shelving. A powder room need be only a vanity with a mirror and the right accoutrements. That often-wasted space under the stairs is the right size for a home bar or a built-in cabinet for storage.

Another small space that deserves your

consideration is the closet. Think of this as a place to show off, rather than to hide with a closed door. Use attractive storage items, such as wicker baskets, which are inexpensive and easily available. Instead of stuffing your clothes in and shutting the door, make the closet an inviting place, where choosing what you wear is a pleasure rather than a chore.

In many urban dwellings with little room to spare, the kitchen itself has become a nook, where appliances are downsized and squeezed in for optimal use. Many of the best appliance manufacturers now make everything from gas stoves to mini-fridges to conform to these tight spaces, and they're just as state-of-the-art as the larger-scale versions. A self-contained kitchen can feel spacious if it is well organized, allowing for everything to be easily reached: Dishes can be accessed from handsome plate racks; pans retrieved from a pot rack hung from the ceiling; and salt, pepper, and herbs can be grabbed from a specially made shelf installed near the stove. Stainless-steel baker's racks can be put to good use if you outfit them with hooks for utensils and dish towels and suitably shaped boxes for even more storage.

Many bathrooms have small areas that can be manipulated to maximize space. Consider building useful and decorative shelves around the sink, or add a skirt and store cleaners underneath. If you have the room, think about installing a sink vanity, which provides much-needed surface area for soap, makeup, skin-care products, and a hand mirror.

Many of us wake up with an invigorating shower. Indeed, some bathrooms allow only for a shower. But if you have a bath, try hanging cheerful curtains around it. Add a wooden frame and create a ledge for reading materials, candles, or incense.

ABOVE You'll want to dally in this ample contemporary bathtub, which is tucked under the eaves on the second floor of a home that was once a barn. The freestanding tub with side-mounted hardware, including a large showerhead and a circular curtain rod, can be closed off from the rest of the bathroom when you want added privacy. The mix of earthy wood, slate floors, smooth gray tile, and chrome fittings provides pleasingly tactile contrasts.

PREVIOUS SPREAD Everything is at the cook's hands (and her assistant's) in this Mexican hacienda kitchen with its dual stoves, tortilla grill, and hearth beneath. Easily accessed canisters holding spices, *masa*, and flour line the shelves, which are tucked into a recessed alcove. Specially made racks hold cooking utensils. Perhaps the most fetching element of this kitchen is the distinctive tiles, which can be found at many specialty shops.

spaciousness and cleanliness

White in a bathroom can promote a feeling of spaciousness and cleanliness without necessarily appearing sterile. FAR LEFT Built-in shelves store towels and other bathroom necessities and even display small collectibles. These open shelves are practical for items you'll want at your fingertips. LEFT This ample tub gets an alcove of its own, inviting one to linger. The wooden frame has a substantial ledge, which provides extra surface space for bath accessories. RIGHT This freestanding bathtub with claw feet gets a welcome revision with a coat of cobalt blue paint. A collection of blue-and-white china and blue-embroidered and -monogrammed towels complements the tub. The towel rack also serves as a partition between the tub and the toilet.

A pedestal sink is a good choice in a cramped space as it uses less area than a vanity sink. Here the ample window ledge provides enough area for a mirror, brushes, combs, and other beauty supplies, and even two delightful Greco-Roman–style busts. Swagged floral drapery and indigo-washed walls contribute to this bathroom's fanciful feel.

The bathtub was once a portable affair. Although it lacked the convenience of modern plumbing, imagine the delight of bathing next to a fire. RIGHT You can re-create this feeling by outfitting an antique copper tub with modern fixtures like wall-mounted faucets. Keeping the tub shiny will take some work.

LEFT Over time, however, copper will develop a smoky patina, which is equally appealing. Be sure to complement the old-fashioned look with the proper accoutrements, such as candles and a tub tray.

The old-fashioned porcelain sink gets two treatments. **OPPOSITE** The pipes and plumbing are left exposed, with a soft pillow underneath providing a great snoozing spot for the family dog. **RIGHT** A gingham curtain is draped around the bottom of a salvaged sink to hide cleaning products. This small kitchen also has plate racks over the sink, which can be used for drying. If you're moving into an old house that still has a wonderful old porcelain sink in place, think twice before replacing it with a newer model. Instead, why not refurbish and update the treasure to meet your needs?

ABOVE Few homes being built today offer the convenience of a pantry. These site-specific and carefully measured shelves accommodate everything from oatmeal to olive oil to a well-stocked bar, all within arm's reach of the table. This sort of arrangement requires attention to neatness, but the aesthetic appeal is a worthy payoff. OPPOSITE Farmhouse pantries, like this example from the late eighteenth century, were once fundamental to food preparation. Large cabinets under the counters were used for storing flour and cornmeal, and the shelves housed dry or canned foods produced from the fruits of the garden and preserved for winter use. Now this pantry nook is used to display antique collectibles, such as crocks, pewter, pitchers, and old apothecary bottles. The U-shaped arrangement of the shelves makes them a perfect installment for the end of a large hallway.

LEFT A contemporary kitchen island with a stove means easy maneuverability in this urban kitchen. The walls accommodate niches that display symmetrically organized bowls and glasses. In this compact arrangement, there is even space along in the wall for a wine rack. The clean and spare lines of venetian blinds, which let in accentuated beams of light, integrate well with this interior. OPPOSITE An old hearth can be updated to accommodate a state-of-the-art stove and matching stainless-steel counter tops. A niche within a nook, the industrious pasta sink has a self-contained boiler and colander. Warm celery tones are a nice contrast to the cool steel of the equipment.

LEFT AND BELOW Here are two efficient, utilitarian, and very handsome solutions to what to do with that angled, awkward space beneath a staircase. Custom-built chests of drawers and shelving have been sized to fit right into the triangle, providing the extra storage that every home needs.

A collection of keys and hat stands, black-and-white photos, subtle wallpaper on one side, and soft oyster gray tones throughout gives this walk-in closet ambience. A painted bureau with burnished silver hardware and shelves, installed on the right, stores everything from clothes to books, suitcases, and cigars. With a closet as inviting as this one, you might just want to hide there and read.

You don't need a lot of space to enjoy the luxury of a dressing table. OPPOSITE This closet has been transformed by the addition of a pink vanity, which once had a life as a desk. Gingham-covered corkboard is perfect for hanging a fabulous collection of evening bags and beads. RIGHT An elegant dressing table positioned at a window is the perfect spot for perfume, brushes, and other keepsakes. Abundant but small-scale drawers provide space for organizing makeup, hair accessories, jewelry, and other personal effects.

Finding a space for a bar in your already overburdened kitchen can be a challenge. Why not convert that seldom-used space under the stairs? Here are three very different approaches. BELOW A custom-made bar is charged by a tangerine and lime color scheme, which is doubly impressive set against high-gloss black paint. The ceramic tile bar top is water-resistant, and a sensible yet aesthetically pleasing choice. There's even an outlet for a blender to mix up drinks and smoothies. Niches are cut out underneath for storing and displaying provisions.

ABOVE A barely finished pine landing houses not only a little bar area, but also a temperature-controlled mini–wine cellar. RIGHT Custom designed for a timber-frame house, the unique shape of this bar adds architectural interest to the room. The raised-panel cabinets provide display niches, used here for bottles and a telephone. A small sink was judiciously installed. Cheers.

Because of changing lifestyles, many people work from home, making an office nook increasingly desirable. If you have the space, you can designate an entire room for this purpose, although, depending upon your needs, this is often unnecessary. A corner, a wall, the end of a hallway, or a landing can provide a great nook in which to create a productive work area.

The minimum requirements are adequate surface space, shelves, a place for filing and storage, and good lighting.

While some people can be productive in a hub of activity, most of us want a place that is tranquil and conducive to work.

Think about the amount of time that you will spend at this workstation. If you have a family and need only a few hours a day to work, a desk tucked into the end of a kitchen counter is probably sufficient. If you require longer hours of quiet time, consider an alcove or hallway that is not heavily trafficked. Keep in mind that natural light might not be available in such a location, so you'll want to make sure to install proper lighting. Recessed down lighting on a dimmer is a good choice for a work area, as it provides plenty of light and can be adjusted as necessary.

The bedroom, which is normally quiet during the day, might be a perfect choice for creating a work space. You can install a desk and some shelves in an unused corner. Make sure you select furniture that will complement the rest of the room rather than make it feel like an office; you still want your bedroom to have an inviting ambience and to look attractive.

Maybe all you need is your own little table for writing letters and paying bills, although chances are you're going to want a computer in your work space. Make sure you have the electrical and DSL capacity that you require. Rather than have cords and wires running all over the place, you should find a location near an electrical outlet, or, alternatively, call an electrician to install the necessary wiring.

Above all, a work area should be a place that will inspire and motivate. For some, that means being able to look up and glance out a window; for others, a window is an inevitable distraction. If you're not someone who thrives in the midst of clutter, make sure you have enough shelves and storage space to organize your belongings.

For those of us who enjoy sewing, having a separate sewing nook enhances creativity. Rather than having to pull out the heavy machine and make room on the kitchen table, you should set an area apart with all the necessary trimmings in place. Proper storage, lighting, and surface space for your machine and for spreading out patterns is all that is required. Find the right corner, hallway, or unused window and you have a sewing nook.

ABOVE A small and unobtrusive workstation has been inserted into this modern room. A simple, rounded shelf serves as a desktop with shelves built in above. A phone has been conveniently installed, and there is room for a laptop computer, if needed.

PREVIOUS SPREAD A quiet place at the top of the stairs with good lighting, both natural and artificial, provides a serene setting for this home office. A pared-down secretary desk is a good choice for such a small space, not only because of its size, but also because of its many drawers and niches for stashing papers, letters, stamps, and other necessities.

In many homes, the master bedroom has become a multipurpose
room. If you're going to create a
work space here, it is important
that the design work with the style
of your room. Typical office furniture, while convenient, will not
blend well with most bedrooms.
LEFT This work space is a suitable
fit. The unobtrusive desk is a
polished wood tabletop mounted
on brackets; the shelves are painted
board. The pretty and versatile
wicker chair is easily integrated
with other furnishings. **OPPOSITE**
An ornate French secretary with
many useful drawers and cubbies
is a good choice for this formal
bedroom. The hinged top can also
serve as a vanity table.

Up in the rafters doesn't necessarily mean dark, as demonstrated by these sunny work areas. Here two L-shaped desks, which provide plenty of surface area, have been installed in the recesses under the windows. File cabinets have been slipped behind the bookcase and another broad work surface has been fitted on top.

A desk is a perfect fit for this window alcove. If you have any uniquely shaped alcoves in your home, they might be just the right size for a work area. Desks come in all shapes and sizes, and are readily available at thrift shops, flea markets, and home furnishing stores. Even if your profession doesn't necessitate a home office, a private place for writing letters or talking on the phone is a welcome addition to any home.

If the kitchen is the center of operations in your home, it might make sense to set up administrative headquarters there by building a work space along one of the counters. LEFT In this kitchen, the computer and monitor can be pushed back, the keyboard tray tucked in, and the chair pulled away when the surface is needed for other tasks. If you enjoy cooking, this convenient work space allows you to quickly look up recipes and ideas on the Internet. You will, however, have to be especially vigilant about spills and other kitchen disasters with this kind of arrangement. OPPOSITE In this kitchen, a counter space extends around the corner to allow for a writing desk that is still part of the kitchen, but out of harm's way.

OPPOSITE This serene home office once had a life as a garden shed. Now it's a quiet place for work and contemplation, although the diverting scenery of the garden might prove to be a distraction. In the winter months, a good and safe space heater is required. ABOVE Once a garage, this efficient home office has been outfitted with ample work surfaces, plenty of storage space and filing areas, and both general lighting and task lighting. During the day, the room gets plenty of natural light streaming through the French doors that replaced the original garage doors.

OPPOSITE The area under the stairs is put to good use in this space-saving work area, with built-in cabinets made to fit. All the drawers and cabinets have low-voltage lighting that turns on when they're opened, illuminating otherwise dark areas. The desk takes the place of honor next to the window. The stairs are maple and stainless steel. BELOW An unused landing or the end of a hallway can serve as a work area, even in such a small and compact space. If all you require is a place to do a little writing or pay some bills, such a space would be perfect. A simple ledge was placed under the window, which provides ample light during the daytime. A sconce provides light for evening tasks.

A sewing nook finds a perfect home in the dormers of the attic in a late-nineteenth-century home. The classic treadle sewing machine still works. The darkly stained floor sets off the delicately patterned wallpaper. Dressmaker forms wear antique lace undergarments, further completing the look.

When creating a sewing nook, light is an important consideration, along with work surface and storage space. LEFT In this bright alcove, the shelves have been outfitted with plastic baskets, which can found at any department store. Coming in all colors and sizes, such containers will fit your specific requirements, whether they are for storing patterns, needle and thread, or fabrics.

light, work surface, storage space

RIGHT A built-in table with drawers below and shelf space above is home to a vintage Woodcrest sewing machine, which is still in good working order.

An entire home makeover can certainly be a satisfying endeavor, but one way to achieve this satisfaction on a smaller scale is to tackle a more modest space in your home, such as a forgotten ledge, an unused alcove, or some empty wall space that is begging for built-in shelves.

Create an eye-catching mini-tableau with a few carefully chosen objects placed on a landing table. The ends of hallways also provide natural niches for displaying sculptures or special collections. It's also the perfect spot for a small table rescued from a flea market. Paint it your favorite color and keep a vase or pitcher of fresh flowers on it. Finally, frame those family photos that you've been neglecting and arrange them on the table next to the flowers.

Simply tucking a rocking chair or love seat into the area under a staircase makes use of that sometimes awkward space and creates another quiet refuge in your home. After a long day, even the thought of climbing those stairs can be exhausting. Wouldn't it be nice to have a cozy place to rest for a few moments? This nook can also provide a surface area for temporarily placing bed linens, laundry, toys, and other objects that need to go upstairs.

Build a breakfast bar at your favorite window near the kitchen and you have a choice spot for daydreaming while skimming the paper as you sip your morning coffee. This can be as easy as installing a well-proportioned wooden counter and two tall stools.

A screen is a great way to make a space more intimate. Use one to create a special corner for yourself. Decorate it with prints, pin postcards to it from dearly missed friends, or cover it with a favorite fabric. Add an inviting chair and a lamp and you have a delightful reading nook.

PREVIOUS SPREAD A mood can be inspired by the simplest of items. Here a small vase of orange tulips is placed against an eggshell blue wall. The milk-washed floorboards contrast beautifully with the dark wood and elegant design of the banister. If you want to animate a corner in your home, it can be as easy as a well-placed vase of fresh flowers.

LEFT Colorful anemones in a white pitcher on an old washstand table, wooden clogs and a book placed underneath, taupe sheers hanging carelessly on the French doors—the simplicity of these objects betrays the true finesse of the design.

BELOW A Moorish-style arch opens up this room, offering a view through to the bedroom. The other carved-out arch services a small basin. Niches were specially designed in the walls for keeping books. If you're renovating and have the chance to build a new wall, consider creating one that will act as more than a wall—with fitted alcove shelving to hold books, sculptures, and other objects.

Looking for a quick getaway? The owner of this home wanted a quiet place to relax, so he converted his garage into a hunting and fishing lodge. The ceiling and floors have been scrubbed and left in their natural state. Sportsman motifs abound—trophies and a box of fishing lures on the table, deer horns on the wall. A hollowed-out rowboat has been ingeniously outfitted with shelves to accommodate a bar.

BELOW An eccentric menagerie of urns, vases, doggies, and other decorative objects resides on carved-out ledges, spilling down onto the oak writing desk. When arranging any collection, keep in mind that the space around the objects influences how the objects will be perceived.

ABOVE Installed at a sunny window, this adaptable blond-wood ledge with a fitted glass top fulfills a number of purposes. During the day, it is the preferred place for sipping coffee and leafing through a magazine, or enjoying a quick afternoon snack while gazing out the window. At nighttime, it can convert to a bar. The lamp and bar stools date from the fifties.

In some homes, entryways are another architectural element that leave room for embellishment. Here a hallway writing desk is surrounded by an eclectic collection of items. The umbrella stand holds antique canes and walking sticks, while another tall basket contains riding crops and other equestrian equipment. On the desk are a Navajo basket with a collection of spurs and a lampshade with an equestrian motif. The painting of a circus acrobat provides a splendid backdrop.

Places of worship are filled with devotional nooks and many family homes have altars as well. Here a corner in a home near Taos, New Mexico, displays a collection of saintly statuary and paintings, Mexican votive candles, and old photos of loved ones. The look is both poignant and festive.

Even in the most spectacular architecture, one can find cozy spots, like this banquette under the stairs in a Spanish home. Plump white cushions are positioned on a ledge under the staircase, a perfect nook for resting or maybe just for contemplating the eccentric wrought-iron chandelier.

BELOW The compact landing of this staircase is the right size and style for this unique sculpture. The tall skinny lady's whippet wanders up the stairs without her.

ABOVE An arching marble staircase with iron and wood banister comes to a soft landing in this radiant alcove. The brightly painted walls and golden upholstery create an illusion of sunshine. Co-opting a landing not only provides a relaxing retreat in your home, but it might also be the perfect place for displaying art. A jade-colored Chinese garden stool serves as a table, and a wall lamp has been installed for late-night reading.

Making your house feel like a home is essentially a matter of filling it with things that you love—whether they are old, new, inherited, or collected. The simple placement of cherished items under a staircase can feel especially comforting. Here an old rocker is placed next to an antique chest and hanging metal lamp. The weaving and the mask on the wall were collected during travels.

Here, the blue-and-white motif and the portrait feel Dutch, the painted boudoir chair appears French, the tureen English, the dishes Italian—yet all of these elements work together in this wonderfully quirky corner of a kitchen. There are no hard-and-fast rules when decorating and creating a nook, except that you display the items you love in such a way that gives you optimal pleasure.

A screen can create a great little retreat, a place for sitting and relaxing. Here a comfy armchair covered with a well-loved fabric, and a handcrafted pillow thrown on top is enclosed by a simple screen that has been crisscrossed with multicolored ribbons. Postcards, photographs, and magazine clippings have been tacked on or wedged into the strips; a collection of gloves is also flaunted.

A resourceful use of a small landing space is to decorate it with specially selected items. Here on an old trunk is a collection of antique wooden boxes stacked next to a basket of garden flowers. A wooden carousel horse sits in the background. A quilt hangs on the banister above a stack of baskets sitting next to an old vessel.

A small room can function like a larger one with the proper outfitting. Not only can a hemmed-in space provide coziness, but it can also offer the added advantage of having everything within reach. Imagine the inherent possibilities and the benefits that such an intimate and workable area can afford. The wall of books in this library, with its high shelves, is made easily accessible by the built-in stairs.

INDEX